CREATIVE CANDLECRAFT

Joan Ann Unger

GROSSET & DUNLAP

A NATIONAL GENERAL COMPANY

Publishers   New York

All black and white photographs and inside color
photographs supplied through the courtesy of
American Handicrafts Company

Acknowledgments

Few ventures are completed without help and so it is with this book. My grateful appreciation goes to family and friends who were patient and encouraging; to Bob and Bea Taylor, owners of "The Golden Eye," Shop of Ancient Secrets, 3855 Pacific Coast Highway, Torrance, California, 90505, for sharing information about Marie Laveau and for permission to quote her listing of zodiacal colors from their catalog; to the staff of the Ann Arbor library who were unfailingly interested and helpful with research problems; and to my editor, Claire Bazinet, without whose interest, encouragement and advice this book would not have been.

JOAN ANN UNGER

Preface

A thousand years ago candles were used to tell time. The candle was divided into twelve sections, each section to burn for one hour and thus time the passing of a day.

In the seventeenth century, auctions in England opened bidding by the lighting of a candle only one inch high. When the candle was completely consumed and guttered out the bidding was closed.

Today, most of our candles are decorative rather than purposeful. While still usable they have become lovely art creations, and more and more women, and men too, are turning to candlemaking as a fascinating hobby and frequently finding it a profitable avocation as well.

More than one husband-and-wife team has developed an enjoyable and profitable business making, decorating and selling candles. One has only to browse through the candle department of a local store or visit a specialty shop to appreciate the vast variety of colors, shapes, and sizes available in candles today. A closer look at the price tags may make you gasp, yet candles similar to these can be made in your own kitchen for only pennies.

Candlemaking offers something for everyone. A hobby for the one with time on his hands and a creative urge to fulfill; a way to enjoy, for only pennies and the investment of a bit of time and effort, the unusual candle creations that cost many dollars in specialty shops; and for yet others, a profitable sideline or full-time business.

Recently I talked with a retired couple from Illinois who supplement their retirement income by making and decorating candles for sale. They live in a mobile home and have converted one bedroom into a candle workshop. Not only does the business bring in welcome income but it provides a satisfying creative outlet and a shared interest and purpose for days that might otherwise seem long and pointless.

Your candlemaking can be anything you want it to be. A cheerful hobby for chasing away the doldrums, a part-time business to earn a bit of pocket money, a project for children on rainy days, a creative craft for shut-ins and oldsters, a money-making project for scout, church or school groups, a full-time vocation for young or old, or just plain fun.

Whatever your desire you will find the techniques easy to master and the equipment as inexpensive or as expensive as you care to make it. You can start small and branch out, or go into it with a bang and a determination to make an interesting business venture a success.

Whatever your reason for entering this most fascinating field, you will find this book a help and guide to making and decorating a wide variety of candles. May your venture into this land of wax and wick bring both pleasure and profit.

J. A. U.

Brighton, Michigan
August, 1972

Contents

List of Color Plates

I

A marbleized layered candle is interesting.

II

Some molded appliqués are large enough to cover the entire side of a candle, as in this three-tiered mammoth.

III

Different-colored layers of wax make a colorful candle.

IV

Shades of one color make a lovely monochromatic layered candle.

V

The marbleized candle uses up leftover chunks of wax.

VI

Leftover pieces of beeswax cut into disks and stacked together make a striped candle.

VII

Several sheets of beeswax rolled together make an interesting and easy candle.

VIII

Even these simple mushroom candles, from multiple-part plastic molds, require careful sculpting of seam lines.

IX

An unusual shape, this quail candle was made from a rubber mold.

X

The zodiac candle uses several small appliqués on each side.

1

Fables and Fancies

After almost 5,000 years of familiarity and usefulness candles still weave an aura of charm, romance and intrigue that is irresistible to most of us. From earliest times man has endeavored to thrust aside the darkness where frightening, unknown evils lurked and to prolong the productive, comfortable hours of light. Candlesticks, not unlike some of our modern candleholders, were found at Crete and date back thirty centuries before Christ. Candles are mentioned in Biblical writings as early as the tenth century B.C., and an actual fragment of candle dating from the first century A.D. was found near Avignon, France.

Since primitive times fire has fascinated man, and even in its more destructive forms the leaping, dancing, devouring flames can attract and hold us spellbound. It is not surprising, then, that candles with their flickering flames casting eerie shadows on wall and countenance, bringing an atmosphere of love, mystery or gaiety to a room, have gathered to themselves a wealth of folklore, superstition and custom.

Candles have long been linked with both joy and sorrow, with births and deaths, weddings and funerals, and have often been imbued with magical powers to influence and foretell the future. The folklore of candles comes from all cultures and while beliefs are sometimes contradictory, remnants of ancient superstitions still abound in our society today.

Some of the folklore has a basis in science, such as the belief that if a candle is difficult to light, rain is foretold and if it lights easily, fair weather is in the offing. High humidity causing dampness in the wick could explain this, as well as the idea that if you blow out a candle and the wick continues to smoke and smolder, bad weather is predicted, but if the candle goes out quickly the weather will be fair.

Not all beliefs are so simply explained. A bluish flame is said to predict frost. Others say a dim blue flame is caused by a spirit passing and is an omen of death. Earlier cultures were much concerned with foretelling death, and an old Welsh tradition has it that if the lighted candle on a church altar is blown out by a draft or in any way accidentally extinguished it signifies the death of the clergyman. It was believed that if one had to rise from the table to light a candle in order to see to finish eating it was a sign that there would be a death in the family. One can picture whole families bolting their food in order to avoid the fatal lighting of the candle!

To dream of an extinguished candle was believed to mean death, while a lighted one signified birth. If a candle guttered as it burned so that wax ran down the side it was considered an omen of death for the person sitting opposite it or to someone in his or her family.

Primitive cultures were anxious to provide the comforts of life for the dead, and in ancient tombs and caskets are often found items of value to the deceased. A candle was frequently included with these to provide the comfort of light and to guide the person's soul on its difficult way. These cultures believed that evil spirits were afraid of light and could only practice their evil in darkness. Thus came into existence the custom of keeping lighted candles around the funeral bier to frighten away evil spirits. It was also believed that the ghost of the deceased was afraid of light and that the burning candles would prevent him from returning to haunt those he left behind.

In Ireland it was a custom to encircle the casket with twelve candles. Evil spirits could not enter a circle of fire and were prevented from carrying away the dead man's soul. But if one of the candles around a bier should fall it foretold another death in the home within a year.

The number three often carried with it a connotation of misfortune, and there was a widespread belief that it was unlucky, or even an omen of death, to have three candles burning in a room at one time. Two, four or more were fine, but never three. In complete contradiction other folks claimed three candles burning in a room signified a wedding to come, and to snuff out a candle accidentally was also taken for a sign of a wedding.

Equally inconsistent, some people believed that a bright spark burning in the wick indicated visitors while others said it foretold the arrival of a letter for the individual sitting closest to the candle. If you wished to know when the letter would arrive you could wet the tip of your finger with your tongue and touch the spark lightly. If the spark stuck to your finger the letter would arrive in a day or two. Even more specific information could be obtained by lifting the candlestick and knocking on the table with it as you repeated the names of the days of the week. The day on which the spark fell from the wick was the day on which the letter would arrive. If you were fortunate enough to dream of a brightly burning candle you could be assured that you would receive a letter from your love. If this wasn't assurance enough, or the dream failed to materialize, you could use a candle to cast a spell on your lover. The candle was used to represent the absent lover and then, while chanting a rhyme, a sewing needle or pins were stuck into the candle. It was believed that when the candle burned down to the pin the absent or unfaithful lover would be impelled to return.

Those who dabbled in witchcraft and the occult also believed it possible to end a love affair between two people by the use of candles and a prescribed ritual of incantation.

Many of the old superstitions linger on today. An example is the belief that it is unlucky to light three candles with a single taper; this lives today in the reluctance of some to light three cigarettes with one match. It was considered unlucky to allow a candle to gutter out in the candleholder, and in coastal areas such a happening was believed to foretell the drowning of a sailor at sea. Even today families of sailors and aviators often burn candles to insure the safe return of their loved ones.

To leave a candle burning in an empty room was believed ill-omened. If it was left for any length of time a death was expected to follow, with the exception of the Christmas candle.

Legend has it that a light in the window on Christmas Eve would guide the Christ child through the darkness and bring good fortune to the household. A very large candle was lit by the head of the household and after burning all night was extinguished on Christmas morning. It was believed to be an omen of misfortune if the candle accidentally went out during the night. In medieval times a stranger attracted to the house by this light was never turned away in case it might be the Lord Himself seeking shelter.

Another tradition, perhaps the forerunner of our Halloween trick-or-treating, was a ceremony practiced in the early nineteenth century known as Lating the Witches. From 11 P.M. until midnight groups including children and adults went about over the hills carrying lighted candles. A candle that burned steadily during the time foretold a full year free from witchcraft for the bearer. If the candle went out evil was predicted.

Today candles continue to play an important part in our traditions and celebrations. Probably the most common is the birthday cake, lighted with candles to honor the recipient and bring good fortune through the year. This custom goes back to the ancient Greeks, when worshipers of Artemis, the goddess of the moon and hunting, brought honey cakes to the temple altars on the sixth day of each month, her birthday. These cakes were round like the moon she represented and were lighted with tapers.

The custom reappeared in the Middle Ages among German peasant families, who used lighted candles on birthday cakes. The candles were lit the moment the birthday child awakened and were kept burning until the cake was eaten at the family meal. Here began the custom of using a number of candles equivalent to the age of the child and an extra one to represent the light of life. Even as today, if the candles could be blown out with one breath, the birthday wish would come true and a happy year was predicted.

Almost all cultures have their own special traditions utilizing candles to enhance and enliven their celebrations. People in the Philippines celebrate the candle dance, in which a girl waltzes about and chooses her mate while flourishing a candle. Western churches honor the Virgin Mary, and Eastern churches commemorate the presentation of Jesus in the temple by candlelit processions celebrating the festival of Candlemas on February second. Moravian churches celebrate the birth of Jesus with their Candle Love Feast on Christmas Eve. Families attend church together, and brown buns and steaming coffee are served during a service of singing. The worshipers eat together in brotherly love and then each is given a beeswax candle to light and hold high as a reminder that each person must be a shining light for Christ.

Churches long insisted upon the use of pure beeswax candles because bees were believed to be from paradise, and today beeswax continues to be used because of its superior burning qualities.

Perhaps the loveliest of candle customs alive in our country is seen in Albuquerque, New Mexico, each Christmas Eve, when special tour buses are provided so visitors to the city can enjoy the amazing spectacle of luminarias. The origin of the custom is not certain; some say it goes back to the Moors of Spain, while others claim the Tortugas Indians originated the custom. However, today on Christmas Eve in Albuquerque you can see entire neighborhoods illuminated by rows of luminarias along walks, driveways, even roof tops. The luminarias are created by folding down the top of an ordinary brown paper bag to make a cuff to stiffen the bag. The bottom of the bag is filled with an inch or two of sand, and a squat, round candle that will not tip over is secured in the sand. When lighted, the candle flame is protected from wind by the bag, and the flickering lights glowing through the paper create an awesome sight throughout the night as the candles slowly burn down and are finally extinguished by the sand.

Many families find special joy in creating their own traditions for celebrating birthdays, holidays and special events, and candles, more often than not, take a place of importance in the celebration. How much more meaningful such customs become when the candles used have been made especially for the occasion by the loving hands of someone in the family.

Perhaps that someone will be you.

2

What You Need
and Why

Even the most elementary candlemaking requires some equipment and a place to work, although your facilities can be as simple as a corner of your own kitchen or as elaborate as a specially constructed room or building. You must provide a work table, a means for melting wax (a hot plate will do), and something to protect your work surface and floor (newspapers are best). Hot running water is a convenience although not a necessity.

Many embark upon candlemaking with only a block of paraffin, a bit of string and some crayons to provide color. They usually find their efforts less than satisfactory. If handmade candles are to burn as well and as long as those commercially made, it won't do to use just any old wax, wick, scent or color. Candlemaking hobbyists who have taken time to learn the best way to make candles find their products often burn even better and longer than commercial ones, and consequently their work is in great demand. Whether you want to make candles for gifts, for sale or simply for your own use, you need to know something about the properties of wax and wick in order to produce a fine, even-burning candle that holds its shape in spite of warm weather and does not drip or smoke.

Paraffin is the wax that most people consider first when they plan for candlemaking. But used alone it does not have a sufficiently high melting point to make it really satisfactory. Candles made from pure paraffin burn too quickly, soften out of shape with the least warmth and are difficult to remove from molds. Wax for candles must be specially formulated and is often available in hobby or craft shops. The large petroleum companies sell wax (a by-product of the petroleum industry) with a variety of melting points. A list of candle supply houses is included in Chapter 9. Remember that wax is heavy and shipping will add considerably to the cost, so a source nearest your home is best.

If you are unable to obtain the prepared candle wax you can use paraffin by adding stearic acid (available at pharmacies and at candle supply houses) or another type of wax with a higher melting point. Formulas are not rigid, and there are many combinations that will make suitable candles. To begin with you might try one of the following:

1. Paraffin—16 ounces; Stearic acid—8 ounces

2. Paraffin—16 ounces; Stearic Acid—9½ ounces; Beeswax—1½ ounces

3. Paraffin—16 ounces; Beeswax—17½ ounces

You may want to try some formulas of your own or experiment with other types of wax with very high melting points such as Carnauba or Candelilla, which are expensive to buy but which need be used only in very small amounts, no more than two to five percent of the total mixture.

If bayberry bushes are found in your area you may make delightfully fragrant candles by collecting and washing the bayberries. Boil them in water until the wax rises to the top, then set it aside to cool and harden. When hard, skim the wax from the top, melt it down again and strain to remove debris. Repeat these steps until all the wax has been boiled from the berries. Bayberry candles are much treasured during the holidays and can also be made by coloring and scenting ordinary candle wax so it resembles the natural product in color and fragrance. An old rhyme is often placed in the bayberry candle package and goes like this:

> *Bayberry candles, burned to the socket,*
> *Bring luck to the hearth and wealth to the pocket.*

When you purchase wax consider the type of candle you intend to make. Some companies offer a variety of melting points ranging from 125 to 140 degrees or higher. Use the higher melting points for candles to be made in metal molds or for hurricane candles. Use the lower melting points for candles to be made in plastic molds or for the votive candle to be burned inside the hurricane candle.

Beeswax can be purchased in sheets, either solid or honeycombed, about eight by sixteen inches and available in a wide variety of colors. Chapter 6 is devoted to candles which can be made from these sheets.

If your candles are to burn well they must not only be of the right kind of wax, but must also have suitable wicks. Plain twine or string is not satisfactory, although you can prepare wicks from these if you wish. Soak the string in a solution of one cup water, two tablespoons borax and one tablespoon salt for several hours, then hang the string up to dry. Impregnating the string with these chemicals slows down the burning process. When the wick burns too fast or is too small for the size of the candle, the wax melts faster than the flame can consume it and excessive dripping results. If the wick is too large the candle does not melt fast enough, there is not enough wax supplied for the needs of the flame and the result is a candle that smokes excessively.

Wicking is available at candle supply houses and is quite inexpensive. It generally pays to purchase a supply in various sizes and types. Most commercial wicks are braided from three strands of threads and form a flat wick which bends over as it burns. This permits the tip of the wick to obtain oxygen from the air and improves the burning quality of the candle.

Wick size is determined by the number of individual threads braided together to form the completed wick. Most wicks are 15, 24 or 30 ply. That is, they contain a total of 15, 24, or 30 individual threads. The threads are divided into three groups and braided. For example, a 15-ply wick will have three groups each containing five threads, the 24-ply will have three groups each containing eight threads. You simply separate and count the threads if in doubt as to size and follow this table for determining the size wick you need for each candle:

15-ply wick . . . . . . 1- to 3-inch-diameter candles

24-ply wick . . . . . . 3- to 4-inch-diameter candles and regular-sized tapers

30-ply wick . . . . . . Over 4-inch-diameter candles and very large tapers

Round wicking, another type, is used for rolling candles from the sheets of beeswax mentioned earlier. Wick with a wire core is made to be used with a small, metal wick holder. The holder has a tab to grasp the wick and is then placed in the bottom of a mold such as a small glass, bottle or other solid object in which it is not possible to make a wick hole. Because of the wire core the wicking stands erect without support (unless very tall) and the wire melts away as the candle burns. This type of wick is often used for small votive candles such as are used in churches and inside the hurricane candle shell.

After wax and wick we usually think of color for our candles. The novice candlecrafter often turns to crayons for coloring candles and then is disappointed when the colors fade or the candles burn improperly. Most crayons contain preservatives that cause wicks to deteriorate so it is much better to purchase professional candle dyes. They come in powder, wax or liquid form, are reliable, easy to use and relatively inexpensive, as they are very concentrated and a small amount goes a long way. Using only red, blue and yellow dyes you can blend them to make almost any color desired. If you remember the color wheel you will recall that:

> Red and blue make purple
> Blue and yellow make green
> Yellow and red make orange
> Yellow, red and blue make brown

Increase the amount of yellow to make chartreuse, increase the blue to make turquoise. Experimenting with color combinations is endlessly fascinating, and by varying the amounts of each color you can make all the shades in the rainbow and then some. A good way to test for color intensity is to drop a half-teaspoonful of the colored wax onto a cold, white plate or saucer. It will harden quickly and you can get an approximation of what the color will be when the candle is hard.

Just as professional colors are best, professional scents are best too for making candles smell as attractive as they look. Perfumes, colognes and toilet water are usually made with an alcohol or water base which will not blend with wax. Perfumes with an oil base may work but they are extremely expensive and not always reliable because they sometimes vaporize rapidly and the pleasant scent disappears.

Professional scents come in a wide variety, and only a small amount is needed to scent a candle. Remember to add the scent just before pouring the melted wax into the molds because overheating may destroy or distort the scent. One-fourth to one-half teaspoon per pound of wax is usually enough.

Additional equipment for candlemaking is easily found about the home. In addition to heat, water, a table and newspapers you will want a double boiler, a candy thermometer, a thick wire or one-eighth- to one-fourth-inch-diameter wooden dowel, baking soda, hot pads, paring knife, ice pick or screwdriver, a cake pan, masking tape, scissors, pencil, wicking, scents or colors as desired, pillow case and hammer to break the wax slab, and molds.

Some of the equipment can be improvised. For instance, you may use an old pan for the base of your double boiler and prefer to use large juice cans (the forty-six-ounce kind) to melt the wax in. Molds may be made from tin cans, jars, glasses, bottles, plastic dishes and cardboard tubes. More will be said about these in Chapter 4.

Candlemaking has few do's and don'ts. It is difficult to make a mistake for you can always melt the candle down again and start over. But there are a few very important warnings.

NEVER MELT WAX OVER A DIRECT FLAME, except when a temperature higher than 210 degrees is necessary to dissolve crystalline stearic acid in a very small amount of wax prior to blending with a full quantity, and then watch very closely.

Equipment for candlemaking.

NEVER LEAVE THE ROOM WHEN WAX IS MELT-ING and always have a box of baking soda within easy reach in case the wax should catch fire.

NEVER USE WATER ON FLAMING WAXING. Water will only spread the flames. A sprinkling of baking soda will suffocate and extinguish the flames. Should the wax inside the container become ignited somehow, turn off the burner and place a lid on the pan to eliminate oxygen and suffocate the flames.

NEVER CAST MOLDS NEAR AN OPEN FLAME.

NEVER PERMIT SMALL CHILDREN IN YOUR WORKING AREA WHEN YOU ARE MELTING WAX.

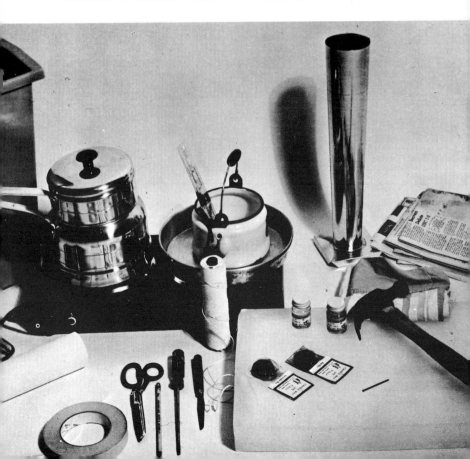

Here then is a list of supplies you will want to have on hand to begin your first candlemaking session.

Wax
Wicking
Scent (if desired)
Color (if desired)
Table
Newspapers
Hammer
Pillow case or bag
Source of heat
Double boiler or substitute with lid
Candy thermometer
Milk carton, other improvised mold

Tea kettle or coffee pot (for pouring wax)
Baking soda
Hot pads
Paring knife or palette knife
Paper toweling
Wire or dowel
Pencil
Ice pick or screwdriver
Cake pan (2-inch sides)
Masking tape
Scissors
Candle mold

Now that you have everything handy let's make a candle!

3

Let's Make a Candle!

When we think about making a candle we most often think of dipping a wick repeatedly into melted wax until layers build up to form a taper. This is still the method used for making tapers, but an easier and more satisfying way to make a candle is by using a mold.

Now that you know the ways of wick and wax and have everything you need at hand, let's put what you have learned into practice by making a candle using the most common of all household objects for a mold—the empty milk carton, quart or half-gallon size.

Milk cartons are probably the most useful and easily obtained molds but they do require a bit of preparation. Be sure the carton is clean and thoroughly dry. Cut the top off with a sharp knife. Because the weight of melted wax is likely to bulge the middle of the carton, it is necessary to reinforce it with bands of masking or adhesive tape at top, bottom and middle. Oil the carton lightly, being careful to remove any excess oil that might cause a bubble in the finished candle. Any light cooking oil is suitable, but select one that will not become rancid at room temperature or you may find your candles developing an unpleasant odor after a time.

Use an ice pick to make a small hole in the center of the bottom of the carton. Measure a piece of wick, considering the proper size for the carton you are using, and allow about four inches extra length. Tie a slip knot in one end of the wick and thread the other end through the hole in the bottom of the carton, leaving the knot on the outside. Fasten the knot to the carton and seal the hole with masking tape or clay so melted wax will not seep out of the hole.

On either side of the top of the carton make a small V-shaped cut and slip a rubber band around the carton near the top. Unbend a paper clip or use a pencil or thin wire and place it across the top of the carton resting it in the V-cut. Drape the end of the wick over the wire or pencil and tuck the end under the rubber band to hold it in place. Pull the wick up snugly so it will be straight in the center of the carton. Now your mold is ready to use.

Once the mold is ready (or even while you are preparing it) you can melt the wax. Place the wax in the pillowcase and with the hammer break the slab into small chunks. Place

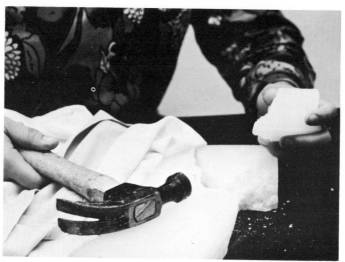

Breaking wax slab into chunks.

Place wax chunks in double boiler.

Use a thermometer when melting wax.

the chunks in the double boiler with water in the bottom and remember to keep a box of soda handy in the event spilled wax catches fire. Use the candy thermometer to measure the temperature of the wax.

When the wax is completely melted remove it from the heat and pour it into the coffee pot or tea kettle. A good pouring spout aids in filling the mold without spillage and helps eliminate bubbles. Color and scent the wax if desired and then, for all paper or plastic household molds, allow the wax to cool until a very thin scum begins to form on the top. Pouring the wax while it is too hot may distort the mold or cause it to burst.

When the scum has formed pour about half an inch of wax into the carton and allow it to harden a bit, then slowly and steadily pour wax into the mold until it comes within half an inch of the top. Pouring too fast may cause bubbles to form in the candle or splash hot wax over the table top and you, so take it slow and easy.

As the wax in the mold cools you will see it begin to contract until a depression forms in the center of the candle. When there is a thick shell of hardened wax and quite a depression in the center of the candle, heat the remaining wax again, to 210 degrees this time.

Using the wire or dowel, and being careful not to slant it and poke through the side, make several holes down through the candle about halfway between the side and the center. This permits trapped air to escape and creates a candle that burns evenly. Fill the holes you have made and the depression in the candle with hot wax and allow it to cool again. You will have to repeat this refilling process several times as the candle cools; it is important so do not neglect it. On the last refilling leave a slight indentation on what will be the bottom of the candle.

It is best to allow candles to cool or "cure" at room temperature, but if you are in a hurry the mold may be placed in the refrigerator. This makes more frequent refilling necessary so watch the candle closely. Complete and slow curing makes it easier to remove the candle from the mold, called "stripping." Allow eight to twelve hours for a candle to cure completely at room temperature and then untie the knot at the bottom of the mold and give a gentle tug on the wick at the top. If your carton was properly oiled and the candle completely cured it should slide out easily. If a candle is reluctant to come out of a mold, placing it in the refrigerator for half an hour may help. Cardboard cartons may be torn away if the candle will not slide out, but placing the mold under hot water should only be used as a last resort and is most likely to ruin your candle. The best way to assure easy removal is proper preparation of the mold and complete, slow curing at room temperature.

Once the candle has been removed from the mold it must be finished or "butted." The bottom edge (which was the top while in the mold) will be rough and sharp. Trim this edge gently with a paring knife to remove the sharp rim of wax, as it is inclined to break off unevenly, leaving an unsightly ragged edge.

A milk-carton candle.

Fingerprints and minor imperfections on the surface of the candle can be removed by buffing with an old nylon stocking or a wax-impregnated, soft cloth, and your first candle is finished.

With few exceptions these are the steps you will use to make any molded candle, so now let us consider the many other household objects that will make suitable candle molds.

4
Molds You Can Make

Your own home undoubtedly abounds with suitable objects to make delightful candle shapes. You must always consider one thing however. Can you get the candle out of the mold?

Obviously a mold with a small top opening and a large bottom would not be suitable unless the container could be broken or torn away. For this reason glass bottles are not usually suitable unless you are willing to sacrifice the bottle. In Chapter 7 we discuss the use of a glass bottle for a candle mold.

Tin cans make suitable molds but you must remember that the upper rim may need to be turned back or removed with tin snips. Some cans do not have rims, but when one is present it makes it almost impossible to remove the candle from the can. Check before you pour and avoid disappointment later.

Paper-towel or toilet-paper tubes make suitable molds although the surface of the candle will be rough and require special finishing. Reinforce the tube even more carefully than you did the milk carton, using masking tape in several places. Trace around the bottom of the tube and cut out a

Remove rims before using tin cans for molds.

circle of cardboard slightly larger than the diameter of the tube. Make a small hole in the center of the circle and cut slits around the edge in the margin you have allowed. Carefully tape the circle to the bottom of the tube, bending the slit sections up around the outside of the tube. Be sure the joint is sealed tightly with tape, floral clay or putty. String a wick through the hole in the bottom and fasten it across the top of the tube just as you did for the milk carton. Placing the tube in a paper cup helps it stand upright and also catches any wax that might leak out.

Pour the mold very slowly and carefully to be sure it isn't going to leak or pop open. Allowing a half-inch of wax to harden in the bottom before pouring the rest will help prevent leaks. As these tubes are very absorbent, oiling the tube is useless, and the only way to remove it is to tear the cardboard away. Bits of cardboard will cling to the surface of the candle but can be washed away with lukewarm water. The candle surface will be rough and will need to be buffed with a nylon stocking or dipped in a hot wax bath, which we will talk about later.

Corrugated cardboard also makes a very unusual candle. Cut a piece of the cardboard to fit smoothly inside a tin can or paper cup, meeting or overlapping just one-fourth inch. Make a hole in the bottom of the can or cup and string, knot and seal the wick as before. When this candle is un-

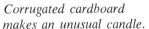

Corrugated cardboard makes an unusual candle.

A paper-towel tube can be used as a mold.

molded bits of cardboard will cling just as with the tube mold and can be corrected in the same way.

Plastic dishes gleaned from your local dairy bar make excellent molds. They come in many shapes, and a wick hole can be made in the bottom by heating an ice pick red hot and then pressing it against the bottom until the plastic melts through. These molds can be used over and over, as candles slip out readily when the mold has been lightly oiled. The finished candle has a smooth, shiny surface.

Use a funnel for a cone shape that makes a good Christmas tree candle. String the wick and then fill the stem end of the funnel with clay or putty. Rest the funnel in a can or jar

while you fill it. The "tree" can be decorated with tiny beads
or touched with whipped wax (see Chapter 8) to give the
effect of snow.

If you plan ahead and serve scrambled eggs for breakfast
you can come up with some dandy disposable molds that
make adorable Easter egg candles. Make a hole in the small
end of the raw egg with a darning needle. Make another hole
about the size of a nickel in the large end and shake or blow
out the contents of the egg. Gently remove any membrane
that clings inside the shell, wash and dry thoroughly. Oil the
shell lightly. Place a bit of tape or clay over the smaller hole
and set the eggshell upright in an egg cup or small glass—or
an egg carton if you plan to make several at once. The wick
can be placed in the eggshell before pouring by stringing it
through the pin hole in the bottom, tying a knot and sealing
the hole with tape or clay, but a more satisfactory method
for these small candles is to place the wick after the candle
has hardened.

Pour the wax as for any other mold but tilt the eggshell
from side to side several times while pouring to prevent air
bubbles from forming along the sides of the shell, which would
result in flat spots or holes in the surface of the candle. Refill as necessary, leaving a flat surface on the top for the
candle to rest upon when finished.

When the candle has completely cured peel the shell away.
To place the wick, heat your ice pick or a metal knitting
needle and melt a hole little by little through the candle,
pouring the melted wax out as you go. Too much pressure
may break the candle so proceed cautiously and let the heat
of the instrument make the hole. When the hole is completed, string the wick through and spoon a small amount
of liquid wax into the hole to secure the wick.

These little candles make delightful Easter table favors
when scented and tinted in pastel shades. They can be
decorated with flowers, sequins, beads, decals or painted
designs (see Chapters 5 and 8).

Gelatin molds make interesting candles. The small, individual molds filled only an inch deep make candles that
float on a bowl of water for a delightful centerpiece. Or make

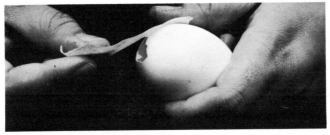

An eggshell is a fragile mold.

Seal the hole in the small end of the eggshell.

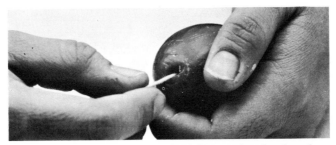

Place the wick in the egg candle after it has hardened.

two halves alike and seal them together with melted wax to make a three-dimensional candle. In these candles too you will place the wick after the candle has hardened. Pieces of small birthday candles work well as wicks for the floating candles. Make a hole with the knitting needle or ice pick and insert the birthday candle, leaving part of it standing above the surface of the molded candle. Fill and seal the hole with melted wax. For the three-dimensional candle carve a groove down the center of the flat side of one wax shape. Using a small paint brush, smooth a thin layer of melted

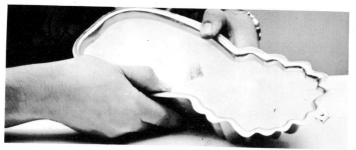

A gelatin mold makes a good candle.

Placing the wick in a two-section gelatin-mold candle.

Place the two half-shapes together.

Smooth the seam line and paint or decorate candle.

wax over the groove and press the wick into place. You will have to work quickly before the wax hardens. Now spoon or brush a thin coat of wax melted to a temperature of 200 degrees over the entire flat surface and press the other wax half-shape into place and hold the two together firmly until the wax hardens. Fill and smooth the seam line, using a paring knife, paint brush and liquid wax, or decorate with glitter. A flat bottom on this or any other candle can be obtained by heating a pie tin and pressing the bottom of the candle on it until enough wax has melted away to flatten the base.

A hollow rubber ball makes a good mold for the snowball candles that are so popular at Christmas. Make holes in the top and bottom as you did for the eggshell mold, the top hole large enough to pour wax into, the bottom just large enough for the wick to pass through. Insert the wick, tie a knot and seal the hole in the bottom. Be careful not to use a ball so large that the weight of the wax pushes it out of shape. And remember to tilt this mold, too, as you did with the eggshell, to prevent air bubbles on the curved sides. To remove, slit gently with a razor blade along the seam line. You may prefer to slit the ball into two halves first, using each one for half of a ball shape as you did with the gelatin molds, and thus be able to use the mold over and over.

A round-bottomed mixing bowl can also be used to make a ball candle by making two halves and sealing them together with the wick in the middle as you did for the gelatin-mold candle. When these balls are covered with whipped wax, sprinkled with glitter and decorated with a few holly leaves and berries they make cherished Christmas gifts. Scenting with pine or bayberry adds even more enjoyment.

Your muffin tin or the little three- or five-ounce paper cups can be used as molds for "blocks" to be joined together to make a fascinating rainbow candle.

Oil the molds as usual but do not string a wick. Melt wax and pour it into each cup to a depth of one and one-half to two inches. Before the wax cools color each cup differently, red, orange, yellow, green, blue, purple. When completely cured remove the colored wax blocks from the cups or tins and make a hole in the center of each one with an ice pick or knitting needle. Make a good-sized knot on the bottom of the wick and string the wick through the candles, setting one atop another in the color order given above. The sections are slanted, so each section will slightly overlap the one below adding interest, or sections can be placed with large and small ends meeting alternately to give an hourglass shape to the finished candle. As each section is set atop the previous one a spoonful of melted wax should be placed between the sections to join them together. When the candle is finished you may want to give it a hot wax bath to complete the joining process and give the candle a lovely, opaque finish.

To do this melt to 230 degrees a quantity of wax sufficient to cover the candle when dipped. Remember that the candle will displace some of the wax so protect your surface in case of an overflow. Dip the candle quickly and set it on a level, flat surface to harden.

You may also want to dip other candles such as the cardboard-tube or corrugated-cardboard candles to give them a smooth finish. When you plan to dip a candle in a hot wax bath it is advisable to leave the wick longer than usual so you can get a firm grip on it. Grasping the wick with a pair of pliers will also help you hold it and keep your fingers out of the hot wax. Candles can be unbelievably heavy when dipping and it is hard to hold on to a stubby end of wick.

If you find you have no container tall enough to use for a wax bath it is easy enough to make one from several tin cans; the forty-six-ounce juice cans are perfect. Leave the bottom in one can but remove both ends of the others, using one or two, depending on how deep you wish to make your container. Solder the open ends together, making one long, cylindrical container out of the several cans. There are liquid solders on the market which do a fair job but be sure to test your seams for leaking before filling with hot wax. If you plan to do much hot wax bathing it is best to have a professional soldering job done on the cans.

Almost anything of metal, glass, cardboard or plastic can be used as a candle mold if you practice a bit of discretion in the selection and preparation of the mold. Glass and metal molds give a shiny, smooth finish. Waxed-cardboard containers impart a softer luster and plain cardboard gives a fuzzy, rough finish which may even add interest to the candle. A fantastic variety of candles can be made using just these things that you find about your home, but sooner or later most serious candlecrafters find themselves turning to professional candle molds.

5

Progressing to
Professional Molds

Professional molds are made of metal or high-impact plastic and come in such a variety of shapes and sizes that it may be hard to decide just which molds are for you. They vary in price, running from under a dollar for a very small mold to as much as fifteen dollars for the very large ones. Many of the plastic molds come in two, three or even four pieces to facilitate removal of the finished candle, and in this way most unusual designs and shapes can be created (see Plate VIII).

When you begin to purchase professional molds consider the possible uses for each mold. Many of the variety shapes are pleasing but have limited potential for decorating and consequently would be of limited use for gifts and for sale. A mold you purchase for four dollars and can only use a few times is not as good an investment as the mold on which you spend ten dollars but which can be decorated in such a variety of ways that you use it over and over again, producing in time fifty or a hundred candles.

When you must decide between two types of shaped or sectional molds you are wise to invest in the more durable product. Flimsy plastic frequently cracks after a time but the newer heavy-gauge, high-impact plastic will take more use and be cheaper in the long run.

Both metal and plastic molds require a bit of care if you are to use them repeatedly for a long time. Plastic molds must be stored away from the heat of radiators or motors, which might soften them enough to cause misshaping. Metal molds must be protected from dampness and rusting. Both should be kept covered and dust free. It is difficult to wash molds thoroughly enough to remove all bits of dust from corners and crevices, yet they will cling to the wax and make spots on your candles.

A silicone aerosol spray available from candle supply firms is an excellent aid for preventing rusting of metal molds and facilitating the release of candles from both plastic and metal molds.

Some molds will come with instructions for the proper wick size but if yours does not, measure the diameter of the candle mold and refer to instructions in Chapter 2. With a candle mold that has many surfaces, such as some of the novelty candles, you will have to judge which diameter is average over most of the candle and determine your wick size from that. Remember that regardless of the wick size these oddly shaped candles will be more inclined to drip and you are wise to burn them only on a protective base (see Plate IX).

Wax temperature is especially critical when using plastic molds. For the softer, clear-plastic molds the temperature should not exceed 155 degrees on your candy thermometer and not over 160 degrees for opaque, white-plastic molds. The newer plastic molds can tolerate higher temperatures, and most molds come with instructions regarding wax temperatures. Follow these carefully so as not to ruin your mold. Refilling of course can be done with a higher temperature because the hot wax does not come in contact with the surface of the mold. Metal molds have the advantage of being able to tolerate a higher temperature of wax, which results in a smoother and more shiny surface.

The sectional plastic molds are formed with bumps on one section and depressions on the other so that you will have no difficulty aligning the parts properly. They usually come with metal clips to hold the edges and bottom firmly together, and mold stands are available. But lacking these you can make do with spring-type clothespins and paper clips placed closely about the edges. Insert the wick in the mold and fasten securely. Prop the mold with jars or bricks.

Metal molds often come complete with a wick holder and a retaining screw or disk to prevent leakage around the wick hole. To prepare the metal mold insert the wick in the small hole in the center of the bottom of the mold. Pull the wick through the mold, leaving wicking protruding from both ends. If a retainer disk has been provided, thread the wick through this and twist it around a nail to secure it. If a retainer screw, twist the wicking around the screw, insert into the hole in the bottom of the mold and screw tight. Pull the wicking up snugly at the top of the mold and loop it around a pencil so the wick is taut in the center of the mold. Seal the bottom of the mold carefully with clay or masking tape to prevent leaking.

Insert wick from bottom of metal mold.

Leave wick protruding from both ends of mold.

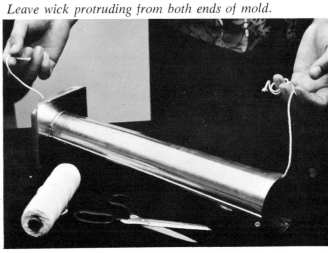

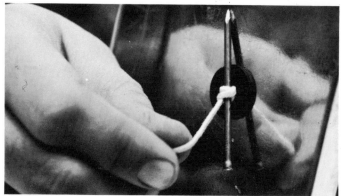

Use retainer disk and nail on bottom of mold.

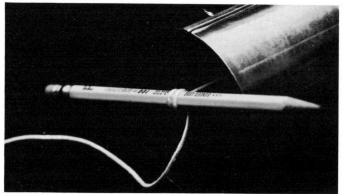

Loop wick around pencil at top to hold taut.

Seal bottom of mold with clay or masking tape.

Remember that molds should always be filled full of wax so that the complete shape will result. When using either type of mold it is wise to stand the mold in a baking pan so that if there should be a seepage of wax it does not run all over. It is also helpful to have about half an inch of cold water in the bottom of this pan to help leaking wax congeal quickly.

Pouring hot wax into cold molds results in a candle surface covered with pinpoint-sized bubbles, as can be observed on most candles for sale in stores today. These defects are easily prevented in your handcrafted candles by heating the mold before casting. This may be done in a very low oven (not over 150 degrees) for about 10 minutes, or by covering the top of the mold with a pad of cloth to prevent water from entering and then holding the mold under hot tap water. Turn the mold carefully so the hot water heats all parts of the outside of the mold. Be very careful not to get water inside the mold. A single drop will make an ugly blemish on your candle.

Working quickly before the mold cools, set it up and fill it with hot wax; 180 degrees is a good temperature. Tapping the sides of the mold gently with your finger will help trapped air rise to the surface. Be careful not to dent your molds at any time and never tap them with any hard object. Even a small dent will make it difficult to remove the candle. Pouring slowly and evenly will also help prevent trapped air.

Refilling should be done the same as with any other type of mold. It is important to stand the mold on a level surface as it cools. A small hand level is helpful for this, as only a few degrees off level will produce a candle that leans. If in spite of your care you should find that the base of your candle is not level you can scrape it gently after it has cured and then smooth it by standing it on a hot pie tin.

The hot water bath (not to be confused with the hot wax bath discussed in the previous chapter) is another way to obtain a smooth, bubble-free surface on a molded candle. This can only be used with one-piece molds and requires a bit of care. First you must have a container large enough so that the mold will sit flat on the bottom, and tall enough so that water will come up as high as the wax level in the mold. A bucket or waste basket is good. If the hot water bath comes up only part way on the mold there will be a difference in the surface appearance of the candle above and below the water line. Use water warm to your hand.

Heat your mold as before, pour the wax, wait about a minute for trapped air to rise, then lower the mold into the water-filled container. Be careful not to splash water into the mold. It may be necessary to weight the mold down with a block of wood or a brick while in the water bath. Allow the water and wax to cool slowly together. This takes longer but it does result in a lovely surface finish. One other caution: be very careful that you have sealed the wick hole tightly or water from the bath will force itself up into the wax in the mold and ruin your candle. When the wax begins to harden and a depression is formed, use your dowel to poke holes as you did before and carefully refill.

Weighting the mold may be necessary with water bath.

Use dowel to poke holes when wax begins to contract.

Refilling prevents air pockets.

Smooth seam with paring knife.

When the candle has cured completely remove the metal mold just as you did the milk-carton mold. When using a sectional plastic mold remove the mold clips and very gently separate the sections of the mold. Forcing may break the mold so pry carefully between the sections. If the candle is stubborn refrigerating for half an hour or so is helpful.

There will be a seam where the sections of the mold were joined. Carefully scrape this seam with a small paring knife or an orangewood manicure stick and buff with a nylon stocking. Be careful not to gouge the candle, and when lines continue over the seam try to reproduce the original design. The end of the orangewood stick, a toothpick or modeling tools are handy for reproducing details on molded candles.

The bottom of these molded candles should also be butted, using a paring knife to remove the sharp edge of wax that may break off and leave an unattractive ragged edge. Plain molded candles lend themselves well to many forms of decoration, and often just the plain candle surrounded by flowers, fruit or leaves is an effective centerpiece.

It is possible to make an interesting *layered candle* of several colors. Pour in the first color as high as you want your finished stripe to be and refill as before, but do not complete the refilling process. Use care not to splash the wax on the side of the mold. When the first color has solidified fairly well poke more holes to complete your refilling process but this time pour the second color of wax on top. The second color will fill in where you have made holes, forming small "pins" of wax joining the two colors quite firmly. A metal mold is best for this because very hot wax can be used each time and the joints will be more secure. Several shades of the same color make a very effective layered candle, or different colors can be used for a rainbow or Mardi-gras effect (see Plates III and IV). It may be necessary to finish this candle with a hot wax bath to cover the lines where colors join, or an interesting effect can be created by dripping wax down the sides of the candle.

Many candles made from professional plastic molds have a great deal of surface detail. To emphasize these details it is often desirable to "paint" over the details left by the mold, such as on a figurine candle. Satisfactory results in this art take some practice so don't become discouraged on your first attempt. The next time you are in a candle shop inspect the commercial candles with painted details and you will find they are usually far from perfect when you look closely. With practice you will be able to do a far better job.

Commercial candle paints are available which are quite satisfactory, but for small items or the infrequent candle that needs a bit of decorating you will find that crayons make an excellent substitute. Painted on the outer surface of your candle they do not interfere with burning. They are a bit more difficult to use than oil paints or special candle paints but a good deal less expensive. Provide yourself with a supply of crayons (broken ones are fine), several fine brushes and an old pan lid with a knob of heat-resistant material. Heat the lid by placing it over a burner on your stove for a few moments. Holding the lid upside-down by the knob, press the crayon of the color you want to use against the inside of the hot metal lid until it melts into a little puddle of "paint." A heavy-gauge lid works best, as it retains the heat and keeps the crayon melted for a longer period. You may also keep a pan of hot water handy and place your lid over this (still upside-down) to keep the crayon in a liquid state. The plain wax crayons often prove more suitable for candle painting than the better crayons with additives, which tend to make the wax grainy.

Working quickly, dip your brush into the melted crayon and "paint" the color on the desired area of the candle. When the color on your "pallet" hardens melt it down again over the pan of hot water. You can use up bits of wax and wax scrapings in this same way although the colors will not be as vivid as those from crayons.

The variety of painted decorations need not be limited to candles with molded designs. If you are artistic you can paint flowers, scenes and decorations on flat surfaces of candles too. The small egg candles are delightful when a spray of lily-of-the-valley, a daffodil or a couple of tulips are painted on the side, and these are very easy to do. You can also paint on trims of gold, highlight curlicues in the molded candle or

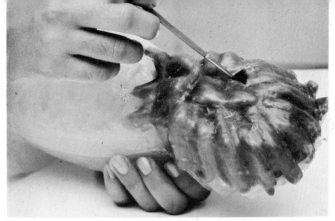

"Painting" candles helps make them realistic.

make bands of color. You are limited only by your imagination and the time and patience you are willing to devote to perfecting this particular skill.

Making molded candles provides unending variety, but for those days when you just don't feel up to the mess of melting wax, hot water baths, etc. there are some equally lovely creations that can be made easily, quickly and simply from sheets of beeswax.

Painting or antiquing curlicues and raised portions of candles adds beauty.

Artistic persons can paint flowers, scenes and decorations on the flat surfaces of candles.

I

II

III

IV

V

VI

VII

When working with beeswax it is best to work in a room where the temperature is about 80 degrees. This makes the beeswax easy to handle and helps the layers adhere to one another. Beeswax candles are an excellent summer project when you have no desire to melt wax over a hot stove and add to a temperature that is already soaring.

The first beeswax candle you will make is the *taper*. Using a full sheet of beeswax and scissors or knife, score the sheet diagonally from corner to corner. Using either scissors or a knife cut the sheet on this line, being careful not to break off the corners. Now you have two triangular pieces of beeswax. Place one piece on your breadboard, leaving about one-quarter inch of the longest straight edge extending over the side of the board. Carefully and very gently so as not to break it, bend the beeswax over the edge of the board. When the entire edge is bent turn the sheet of wax over so the bent edge stands upright. Place the wick, cut an inch longer than the beeswax sheet, along the fold in the wax. Keep the wick almost even at the bottom edge and allow it to extend above the point, which will be the top of your taper. Gently again, bend the folded edge of beeswax over the wick securing it firmly. Now slowly roll the long edge of beeswax toward the diagonal cut edge, being careful to roll evenly and tightly. When you have rolled the entire sheet you will have a graceful taper about sixteen inches tall.

You may leave the taper as it is but a graceful fluted edge can be formed by using your thumb and forefinger to gently flare out the cut diagonal edge of the beeswax as it spirals down the candle. Trim can be added to the edge as you flute it by dipping your fingers into glitter and pressing them against the wax. Beeswax has a naturally sticky texture so glitter adheres well without the use of glue.

Straight *cylindrical candles* are made with a rectangular piece of beeswax. You may use a full sheet of beeswax and roll from the short edge for a fat, squatty candle, or roll from the longest edge for a tall, slim candle. This candle is rolled just as is a taper, by first bending the edge over your board, then inserting the wick and finally completing the rolling, being careful always to roll as tightly as you can to exclude as much air as possible. Seal the edge against the candle by pressing gently with your fingers.

Experiment by using different-sized rectangles. Soon you will be able to judge the proper-sized rectangle of wax to use for just the height and diameter of candle you wish to make.

The cylinder candle may also be made using more than one sheet of beeswax. Using the first sheet make a cylindrical candle as before. Do not press the edge down but butt the edge of the next sheet up against it tightly and begin rolling sheet two around the core made with sheet one. Any number of sheets may be rolled together this way. When you have finished press the edges together and mold the candle with your hands until the warmth has sealed the candle together.

For an interesting *two-tone candle* use beeswax cut diagonally as for the taper, but use two sheets of contrasting or blending colors. Place one sheet on top of the other with the diagonal edge of the top sheet extending about one-half inch beyond the diagonal edge of the bottom sheet. Begin rolling (after bending the edge of the bottom sheet and placing the wick as before) and catch the top sheet in as you roll. Complete rolling the two sheets together. This finished candle will have a two-color spiral edge circling down for a most interesting effect. You can leave the candle as it is or flare either or both the diagonal edges and trim with glitter.

The same procedure can be followed using two rectangular pieces in two or more colors for a cylindrical candle with a stripe down one side. An interesting effect is created by cutting a design along the outer edge of each sheet (see Plate VII). Mold the edges firmly with your hands. As these multi-tone candles burn, the colors will show in the drippings for an unusually lovely effect.

Adorable little *Christmas tree candles* suitable for table favors are easily made using dark green beeswax. Measure, score and cut one full sheet of beeswax lengthwise into four strips. Beeswax sheets vary in size from one manufacturer to another. The sheets may be seven and half to eight inches in width, fifteen to sixteen inches in length so it is always best to measure and divide evenly.

After dividing you will have four strips approximately two

by sixteen inches. Score each of these strips diagonally from corner to corner as you did when making the taper and cut again. You now have eight long, thin triangles. Place a wick cut about two and a half inches long against the *short* straight edge and roll from this edge to the point, making a squatty little tree shape. Decorate with glitter or tiny glass beads and top with a tiny sequined star. Any size Christmas trees you desire may be made by varying the size of the triangle.

An attractive candle that lends itself to many forms of decorating is the *tiered beeswax candle*. Use a rectangular piece of beeswax about eight by ten inches. Cut another full sheet into two equal pieces about eight by eight. Using the larger piece and placing your wick on the long side roll a cylindrical core which will be about one inch in diameter and about ten inches tall. Now roll one of the eight-by-eight-inch pieces around the first cylinder, keeping the bottom edges even. You will now have a candle with a center about ten inches high, then a step about eight inches high. Cut the remaining eight-by-eight-inch piece into two four-by-eight-inch pieces. Again, keeping the bottom edges even roll one of these around the candle. Butt the edge of the second four-by-eight-inch piece against the edge of the first and roll it around too. When you are finished you will have a three-tier candle with "steps" which are fun to decorate. The candle can be made in one color or in several, and different sizes and proportions are easily made and decorated to represent miniature wedding or anniversary cakes. Pieces of beeswax left over from other candles can be used up in this candle too.

Another way to use up odds and ends of beeswax sheets is to use a cookie cutter to cut round disks about two and a half to three inches in diameter in a variety of colors. With your ice pick make a hole in the center of this first disk. Insert a length of round wick and tie a slip knot to hold it firmly against the disk of wax. Now, one by one, place a hole in the center of the other disks and string them on the wick, stack them evenly and press each one gently on top of the previous one as you work. When the candle is the desired height it can be dipped in a hot wax bath to secure all the disks firmly together. Or if you prefer you can, as you place each disk on the wick, pour a spoonful of melted wax between each one to bond it to the next. Either the solid sheets or the honeycomb design can be used for this candle (see Plate VI).

Realistic-appearing *cat-tail candles* are made using a full sheet of dark brown beeswax. Bend the edge, place the wick and roll a cylindrical candle from the short side of the sheet. With fingers and hands mold the top and bottom of the cylinder until the ends are rounded like a cat-tail. Use wooden dowels painted green or colored with food coloring for the stems. Cut long, green leaves from a sheet of beeswax and mold them around the stems. If the beeswax is too flimsy to stand erect alone press two leaf shapes together and mold the edge with your fingers to thin and seal them. Arrange three or four "cat-tails" in a tall vase or on a plastic-foam base for an effective centerpiece. Smaller cat-tails can be made by using smaller rectangles of beeswax.

Attractive *fruit candles* molded of beeswax make unusual centerpieces also. Form a squat or cylindrical candle roughly the size of the fruit you wish to mold. Shape it by pressing and squeezing with your hands and fingers until the desired shape results. Realistic apples, pears, peaches, bananas, and plums can be made this way.

Calla Lilies made of beeswax are lovely at Eastertime. Using the pattern given here make cardboard patterns of your own. Mark and cut two petals from white beeswax. Using a piece of yellow beeswax about seven by eight inches cut into a triangle, make a taper about seven inches high with a wick in the center. Press the two petals together firmly and pinch the edges to seal and thin them. Gently shape the petal around the taper. If the wax is too brittle to mold easily it can be softened by dipping briefly into warm (not hot) water. Use a dowel for a stem and cut leaves from green beeswax. Arrange one or more of the Calla Lilies in a vase or plastic-foam base.

To grace the table for a summer barbecue make beeswax candles shaped like ears of corn. Roll a cylindrical candle of yellow beeswax about eight inches long. Round the top as you did for the cat-tails until the candle resembles an ear of

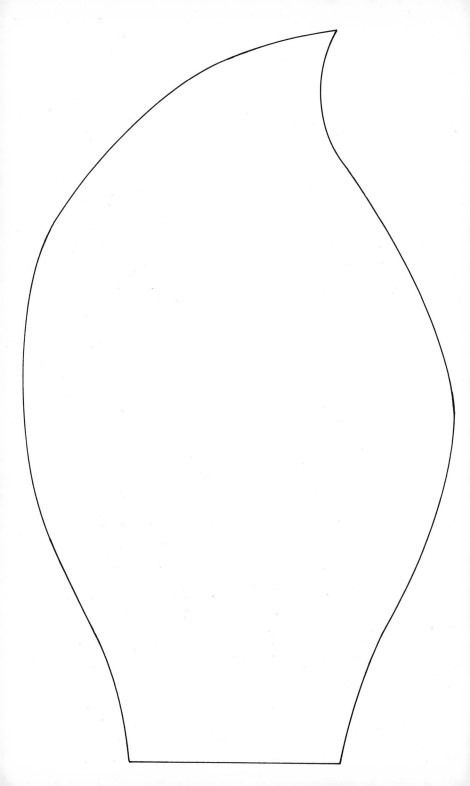

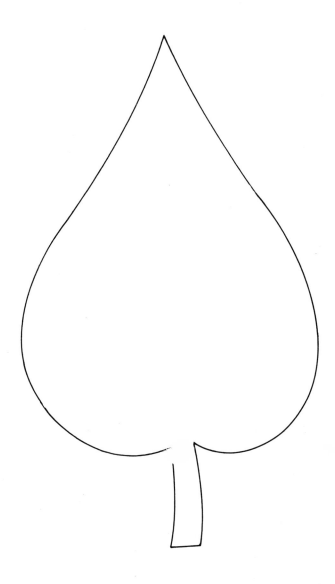

Calla Lily petal and leaf patterns, actual size.

corn. Cut three or four husks out of light green beeswax and shape them around the ear. Bend the tops of the husks outward at different levels to resemble partly peeled corn. You may use bits of reddish or brown wax pressed on to resemble a few individual discolored "kernels" so often found on corn.

Never discard the leftover bits and pieces of beeswax. They can be used in many ways, some of which we will discuss in later chapters.

To give a nice finish to the bottom of your beeswax candles, heat a pie plate or cake tin over a low flame. Turn the flame off and press the bottom of the candle against the hot metal for a minute or two, being careful to hold the candle straight. The melted wax will seal the layers of beeswax together and make a smooth, finished bottom.

Remember that beeswax candles burn faster and drip more than molded candles and may even smoke somewhat while burning. This is because it is impossible to completely eliminate the air contained in the small cells in the honeycomb beeswax sheets and between layers in the solid sheets. Rolling the candles as tightly as possible will help but the problem cannot be completely eliminated. The dripping is quite attractive on the candles but do remember to protect table surfaces when burning beeswax candles.

There is no end to the interesting and delightful candles that can be made using your imagination, and a book of instructions for making paper flowers will provide many ideas and patterns adaptable to beeswax candles. Now let us make some special candles, for special occasions.

7

Special Candles for Special Occasions

One of the most dramatic of all the beeswax candles you might make is the *variegated spiral taper*. It stands almost sixteen inches high, is over three inches in diameter, is stunning in appearance and although it looks difficult, in reality is quite simple to make. The cost for materials is less than three dollars but the finished candle on a suitably decorated base would bring fifteen to twenty dollars in most candle shops.

You will need seven full-sized sheets of honeycomb beeswax, three in a tan color and one sheet each of brown, rust, apricot and yellow. Bend the long edge of one of the tan sheets over your board as you were taught in the preceeding chapter. Place the wick and begin rolling a tall, cylindrical candle. Butt the next sheet of tan against the first and continue rolling tightly and evenly. Butt the third sheet of tan and complete the rolling of the center core of your candle. A cylinder about two by sixteen inches will result. Press the edge down firmly.

Score and cut each of the other four sheets lengthwise into three equal strips about two and a half by sixteen inches.

Without using wicks roll each of these pieces into a long, thin rope about one-half inch in diameter and sixteen inches long when finished. When all are rolled arrange them in the most attractive order, usually brown, rust, apricot, yellow, brown, rust, apricot, yellow, etc., in front of you.

Be sure your work area is warm enough, 80 degrees or over, for the beeswax to adhere to itself best. Carefully place the end of one of the brown ropes against the top of the tan core, keeping the upper edges even. Curve the rope gently to the right as you turn the core to the left until the rope is about halfway down the core. Now reverse the curve, bringing the rope back gently so it almost reaches the bottom. It will probably end up about half an inch above the bottom edge because making the double curve takes up some of its length. The bottom of the rope should come about halfway around the core when it is properly in place with a gentle "S" curve. Press the rope to the core gently but not too firmly so it can be adjusted later if need be.

Continue to apply the thin ropes in turn, placing each one closely against the previous one until all are arranged in concentric curves around the core. The curves must be very gentle if all twelve ropes are to fit properly around the central core. If you reach the end and find the last rope will not fit you must gently adjust each of the others until all slip properly into place. Adjust the ropes until they fit evenly around the core without spaces or crowding. Press the entire candle between your hands, gently warming it until all ropes adhere to each other and the central core. Use a hot knife to cut the bottom of the core even with the ropes around the sides and seal the bottom on a hot tin. A base of wax, whipped or plain, or of plastic-foam and decorated with fall leaves, acorns or miniature fruits makes this candle an outstanding harvest-time decoration (see wax base shown on front cover).

Many other color combinations are effective: dark green, red, white and light green makes a striking Christmas candle. Red, rose, pink and white with a base of roses makes a lovely summertime centerpiece. Any monochromatic color scheme is attractive, and a candle of this sort makes a most welcome gift when made to harmonize with room decor. A particularly lovely and unusual conversation piece was made on order using off-white, gray, aqua and lavender to complement a room decorated in those colors. The variegated spiral taper makes a striking spot of color even without a decorated base and is particularly effective on an unusual holder.

The *cinderella candle* is another special candle that has fascinated the uninitiated for a long time with its dripping colors and swiss-cheese appearance that constantly changes shape while burning. The cinderella candle is really two candles in one, most often made with a core candle of a deep color and a white outer candle. When it burns, melted wax from the inner core drips out through the holes in the outer candle and is fascinating to watch.

The inner candle can be purchased or molded but should be one to two inches in diameter and the same height as your finished candle will be. If you mold this candle yourself leave a long wick on it and don't bother to buff or polish the candle.

The cinderella candle.

You will need a mold three to five inches in diameter. A professional metal mold, milk carton or juice can is good. Prepare the mold as you did before but instead of inserting a wick, place the smaller candle in the mold with its wick protruding from the wick hole. This can be accomplished by tying a piece of regular sewing thread to the wick, carefully threading the thread through the hole and pulling the wick and candle gently into place inside the mold. This is most easily done with the mold lying on its side.

Once the center candle is in place stand the mold on a flat surface. Melt a quantity of white wax and while it is melting prepare a good quantity of cracked ice. Do not crush the ice but crack it into assorted-sized pieces. Too-small bits will melt too quickly, too-large pieces will leave unattractive spaces. Be sure you have enough ice to fill the space in the mold around the inner candle but do not put the ice in the mold yet.

When the wax has melted pour about half an inch of wax into the mold and allow it to harden. This will hold the center candle firmly in place and provide a smooth top surface for the completed candle. Be sure to keep the center candle straight as the wax hardens. When the wax is quite firm fill the space around the candle with the cracked ice to within one-half to one inch of the top of the mold because you want a solid base on the bottom of your candle too. Pour the hot melted wax over the ice slowly, permitting it to run to the bottom. If you pour too fast you may trap too much air. You do not need to refill this candle unless a very large indentation forms on top, and then do not poke. You want holes in this one!

Allow the candle to harden completely at room temperature. When it is completely hard remove it from the mold while holding it over a sink. Shake the candle to remove any remaining water, and if you can see water trapped under a thin film of wax use an ice pick to break open the wax film and release the water.

You may buff the outer surface or dip the candle in a hot wax bath if it needs finishing. Often the edges of the holes are quite sharp and a hot wax bath softens and finishes them nicely.

The *tavertine candle* is another that you have probably admired in specialty shops and wondered how in the world it was made. It is really quite simple once you know the secret.

Select a suitable mold, usually a short, squatty one or a larger one with a diameter of at least three inches. Prepare the mold just as you would for any ordinary molded candle. Once the mold is prepared, crumple pieces of foil into the mold. Ordinary aluminum foil or the colored foils available at Christmas will do. Keep the crumpled foil near the outer edge of the mold and be sure to arrange some so the flat surface of the foil is against the side of the mold where it will show to best advantage on the finished candle. Fill the mold with white or colored wax and refill as before. When the candle has cured and been removed from the mold it will probably need a hot wax bath in order to cover all pieces of foil with a translucent layer of wax. If foil is left uncovered it has a shiny, unattractive appearance and is easily recognized as just plain foil. Covered with a thin film of wax, the foil glows softly and the crinkles and folds make a lovely design on the tavertine candle.

One of the nicest gifts you can make for a family member or a close friend is the *memento candle*. This takes some advance planning so don't decide to do it the night before some special occasion. This candle is to be a remembrance of all the happy occasions at which candles were used. Perhaps the person you plan to make the memento candle for has a birthday celebration. Collect the candles used on his cake or for table decorations. You can begin making the memento candle as soon as you have these or you may label them and put them aside until you have collected samples from several occasions. But do be sure to label them. Half the pleasure in the memento candle is knowing what occasion each color represents.

When selecting a mold for the memento candle remember that the candle will probably incorporate a variety of colors, will have no decorating to speak of and, if you do it little by little, may need to remain in the mold for quite a period of time. Choose a mold that you will not need to use during this time and one that will do justice to such a candle. Interestingly shaped bottles are good for the memento candle or the plastic containers from a dairy or ice cream bar. Prepare the mold and place the wick as before. If you use a glass bottle you may wait and place the wick after the candle is completed or use a wire-core wick and wick holder.

Carefully clean the candle stubs you have collected to remove all bits of smoked wax and burned wick. Melt down each lot separately. Perhaps the birthday celebration candles were a cheerful red. Melt them and pour the wax into the mold, saving a bit for refilling. If you find the wax is dirty when you melt it you can strain it through several layers of cheesecloth. A satisfactory and disposable filter can be made using a length of wire, facial tissues, paper clips and a clothespin. Make a loop of wire about three inches in diameter with a short handle. Wire the handle around a clothespin for a better grip. Place three or four facial tissues on top of each other and press them down into the loop of wire, forming a strainer shape. Fold the edges of the tissues over the wire and secure them with paper clips. Pour the melted wax gently through this filter, being careful to replace the tissues at frequent intervals as they become dirty and before they break through.

Allow the first layer of wax to harden in your mold, making a few holes to permit the next layer of wax to "pin" in place (see Chapter 5). When the first layer is hard melt the candles saved from the next occasion, perhaps some gold ones from Thanksgiving dinner, and pour on top of the first layer, again reserving some for refilling. Continue adding layers until the mold is filled. Unmold as before. If you are using a glass container such as a bottle you may find the container will have to be broken away to remove the candle. This can be done in two ways. Chill the container and candle thoroughly in the refrigerator or freezer, then remove and immediately plunge into boiling water. The rapid change of temperature will shatter the glass. But remove the candle from the water quickly before part of the wax melts away. Or you may wrap the glass container in a cloth and rap it smartly with a hammer to break the glass away. Either procedure involves a bit of risk to you so do be careful. Unusually shaped bottles make excellent molds for the memento candle because they are so different, but they can make this a most difficult candle to complete.

When the candle is unmolded polish it and finish the bottom as you have done before. Give the candle a hot wax bath if needed and present it with a little card listing the colors of the layers and the occasions from which the candles were saved. The recipient will recall with pleasure all the happy occasions this candle commemorates.

After you have been candlecrafting for a while you will find yourself with a quantity of bits and pieces of wax in different amounts and colors. Don't throw them out! Remember those lovely *marbleized candles* you've seen that cost so much in specialty shops? Well, here we go!

Prepare a mold as usual. A metal mold is best for this candle because you can use hotter wax, resulting in a better bond between the filling wax and the marbleizing chunks. Select wax in a contrasting or harmonizing color. If you have several colors of leftover wax make a gay *Mardi-gras candle* by using many colors and filling the mold with white wax (see Plate V). Or make a *marbleized layered candle* by using one color at a time in layer over the chunks (see Plate I). If your leftovers are dark blue try filling with pale blue. Green chunks with pink filling wax is attractive, as is brown and orange chunks with yellow filling. Melt ∾ ever color wax you have selected for filling until the temperature reaches the maximum for the mold you are using, with 180 degrees about the top. Too-hot wax will cause too much melting of the chunks and "muddy" the colors. Fill the mold with the chunks of wax. Don't make the chunks too large or too small but do vary the size and shape of the pieces. Pour the hot melted wax slowly into the mold until all spaces between the chunks have been filled. Release air pockets very carefully and refill as you would with any molded candle. Fascinating color combinations are possible in the marbleized candle and you can even use up scraps of beeswax in these candles. Beeswax has a higher melting point so use a metal mold and pour the wax at 180 degrees.

Another candle that makes an especially nice gift is the *hurricane candle*. In this candle an outer shell of wax is made and decorated as desired. Inside the shell is placed a smaller candle, usually in a glass holder, which burns within the outer shell creating a soft glow through the shell and leaving it and the outer decorations intact. The small inner candle is replaced as needed and the outer candle can be used indefinitely, making it a most suitable souvenir or gift item.

To make a hurricane candle, select a short, squat mold and prepare as usual, omitting the wick. Fill the mold with wax and permit it to cool until about half an inch of wax has solidified. With a sharp knife carefully cut around the top surface about half an inch from the edge and remove the center piece. Pour the rest of the melted wax out of the candle, leaving a shell on the bottom and sides about half an inch thick. Allow the shell to harden completely and remove it from the mold. Trim, butt and polish the sides, top and bottom edges.

Making the hurricane candle shell.

Insert votive candle in center of hurricane shell.

You may purchase small votive candles to burn inside the hurricane candle or make them using small whiskey glasses, brandy snifters or plastic cups for molds. Be careful to center the inner candle and keep the hurricane away from drafts to prevent the flame from softening the outer shell. Be sure to cast your hurricane out of wax with a high melting point and the inner candles out of low-melting-point wax to reduce the danger of melting the outer shell as the inner candle burns. The wire wick and small metal wick holders are easiest to use for making the inner candles.

The hurricane candle lends itself well to many decorations that could not be used on other candles, for the shell does not burn and you may decorate all the way to the top and also utilize materials that would be inflammable and thus unsuitable for regular candle decorations.

Adding these special candles to your collection will greatly enhance your pleasure, but learning to decorate the plain molded candles so they become true works of art will add even greater variety and make possible the creation of a truly endless array of candles.

8

Decorating Makes Candles Dramatic

A tremendous amount of satisfaction and creative pleasure awaits once you begin to enhance plain molded or rolled candles with imaginative decorations. A simple molded cylinder becomes a breathtaking wedding candle with the addition of bells, bows and silver glitter. A simple beeswax taper takes on a garden-party air when you add tiny rosebuds and a butterfly. Tasteful decoration adds beauty and value to your candle creations, and the variations are as endless as your imagination and the materials available.

Whipped wax is perhaps the single most useful technique for decorating candles. To make this you will need melted wax and a fork or egg beater if you have an old one you no longer use. Melt the wax in a container with high sides so it will not splatter when you begin to whip it. When the wax is melted allow it to cool until a thin film forms on top. Attempting to whip wax before it reaches this film stage is useless, as the whipped wax just melts down again and you use a lot of energy needlessly. Once the film has formed begin to whip the wax just as you would whipping cream, using the fork or the beater and continuing until the consistency resembles whipped cream.

Apply the whipped wax to the candle with a fork or your fingers just as you would apply frosting. Or place a candle on a sheet of waxed paper and scoop the whipped wax all around it to create an attractive base for decorating. While the wax is still warm and soft sprinkle glitter or silicate snow over the wax or press decorations into place. Whipped wax makes an especially nice base for Christmas candles, and pressing small Christmas baubles, holly leaves and berries, or artificial poinsettias into the wax base makes an outstanding table decoration. Dollops of whipped wax dropped here and there on the sides of a candle and piled on top give an appearance of snow and make stunning winter candles.

The ball-shaped candle completely covered with whipped wax and sprinkled with glitter is a popular Christmas gift item and so easy to make. You need only press two or three holly leaves and some berries against one side to produce a simple yet lovely candle (see front cover photo).

Colored wax may be whipped also to use as a colored base. You can create ocean waves around a candle to be decorated with netting and seashells. The netting from bags of fruits and vegetables makes a good background for a seashell design and works especially well in the hurricane-type candle where the outer surface does not burn.

A particularly lovely candle that gives the feel of splashing ocean waves can be created using only liquid wax. Make or buy a simple cylinder candle, one to two inches in diameter, eight or ten inches in height. A cardboard-tube candle is good for this. Cover a cereal bowl with aluminum foil inside and out (or use a individual-sized aluminum-foil pie pan). Pour enough wax into the bottom of the bowl to form a base for your candle. Place the candle in the wax and allow the wax to harden around the candle. Fill a container such as a bucket or wastebasket with cold water. When the wax around the candle has completely hardened pour additional wax at 165 degrees into the bowl. Lower the bowl and candle into the container of cold water until the water is lapping around the top edge of the bowl and is supporting most of the weight. Then hold the top of the candle and quickly plunge the bowl, liquid wax and candle into the cold water,

Allow wax around candle in foil-covered bowl to harden, forming a solid base.

Swirled wax attached to candle resembles ocean waves.

twirling the candle as it submerges. The melted wax will rise and solidify in the water, adhering to the candle in a fascinating sweep of shape and color resembling waves crashing on a beach. A base decorated with seashells makes an appropriate addition to this candle.

Another interesting effect is created by dropping small drops of wax on a sheet of waxed paper. When the drops are solid attach them to the sides of a candle with liquid wax for a "nail-stud" effect.

If you have an artistic bent very attractive designs can be carved into or painted on your candles (see Chapter 5). For embossed candles trace the design on a piece of paper and then tape the paper in place on the candle. With a pin or needle trace the design onto the candle by making tiny pin pricks along the lines. A ballpoint pen can also be used to make indented lines on the candle as a guide. Use carving tools, a paring knife, orangewood sticks and toothpicks to carve the candle with designs or initials. When the carving is completed buff the candle for luster and to soften the edges of the carving. Raised surfaces may be brushed with gilt or paint to emphasize the design or a rubbed-on antique finish may be used. The carved-out areas may be partially filled in with another color by dipping the candle quickly into a contrasting-color wax bath and then, working quickly before the wax hardens completely, gently rubbing away the surface wax leaving it only in the embossed areas.

Artificial flowers, either plastic or paper, can be dipped into melted wax and used for attractive decorations. Be careful to dip quickly and allow the wax to drip well so droplets of wax do not harden on the petals. Dry the flowers by sticking the stems into a sheet of plastic-foam or place them in small glasses. Paper flowers may require two or more coats of wax as the first coat is likely to be absorbed by the paper. While it may be tempting to dip a whole bunch of small flowers in one fell swoop, don't try it! The flowers will all stick together in a gooey mess.

A little more difficult method but one that is very satisfying and particularly effective is to make the flowers yourself out of thin sheets of wax. The shaping of flowers requires some practice but these delicate wax creations are well worth the time in the ohs and ahs of admiration they bring.

A marble slab is ideal for pouring out a thin layer of wax, as it holds heat well and will keep the wax at molding temperature for a rather long period of time; you may also use a baking sheet set over another pan of warm water. If you do use a marble slab, wooden sticks placed around the edges of the slab are helpful in keeping the wax from running off.

Roses are most in demand and are fairly easy to make so we will start with them. Make heart-shaped patterns for the rose petals or use heart-shaped cookie cutters in graduated

Shape leaves and petals with your fingers.

Curve petals with your fingers.

Larger flowers with wicks make lovely individual or floating candles.

sizes. You will need several sizes so the inner and outer petals can be made in different sizes from about three-quarters to one and one-half inches in diameter.

Melt enough wax to permit two pourings on your slab or tin. The first pouring will warm the slab, so the second pouring will harden more slowly, giving you more time to work. Pour a layer about one-eighth-inch thick and allow it to remain on the slab for about five minutes, then peel it away and put it aside to remelt and use again later. Now that the slab is warm pour the second layer about one-eighth-inch thick and watch it carefully until it begins to harden. Trace around your patterns on the wax and cut out the pieces with a knife or use your cookie cutters. Allow the wax pieces to become firm but not hard; they must remain pliable or you will not be able to shape the petals. Select the smallest heart shape and roll it loosely with the point down so that the top of the heart resembles the center rolled petal of a rose. Use another small heart shape and roll it around the first. Continue to add petals, gradually using the larger sizes and shaping each petal as you add it. Pinch the edge of the petal to thin it and roll it outward to form a graceful rose shape. Use five to seven petals depending on the size you wish the finished rose to be. Press all the petals firmly together at the bottom and flatten slightly to provide a base for attaching the rose to the candle.

These roses are best attached to the candle with a small straight pin and melted wax. Leaves cut from a sheet of green wax and scored with a toothpick are also shaped with your fingers and attached around the rose with pins and wax.

Many different flowers can be made from these poured wax sheets, and you will find that patterns for making flowers of paper will also work quite well in wax. Just remember to keep the wax pliable, work quickly and shape each petal with your fingers until it is the desired shape.

Larger flowers with a small wire wick or piece of birthday candle in the center make lovely individual place candles on a dinner table, or floating in a dish of water as a centerpiece. Ribbons, bows and streamers can also be cut from thin sheets of wax and shaped by hand into most attractive decorations for wedding, anniversary and Christmas candles.

These candles are especially lovely when trimmed with handmade wax bells. A small bell mold such as is used for making sugar bells for cake decorating is needed. Oil the mold lightly with salad oil, block any hole in the top of the mold with clay and fill with melted wax that has been allowed to cool slightly. Set the bell upright in a small glass, egg carton or block of clay. When a wax shell about one-eighth-inch thick has formed use the tip of a paring knife to gently cut out the center of the layer of wax just as you did with the hurricane candle. Pour out the remaining liquid wax and allow the bell to harden completely. Cool in the refrigerator if necessary to remove the wax shape from the mold. Affix two or three of these bells in a cascade to the side of a candle with pins and melted wax. Add a wax bow and streamers and you have a lovely and unique wedding or Christmas candle.

Leftover pieces of beeswax can be used to make a wide variety of appliqué designs. Simply cut the appliqué shape from the beeswax and press it into place against the side of the candle. The sticky texture of the beeswax will hold it in place without pins, glue or melted wax.

A red beeswax heart pressed against a tall white taper with an edging of gold-lace trim and a base of white whipped wax covered with wax-dipped pink roses says "I love you" for a long time to a special Valentine.

Hands of a clock cut from beeswax and pressed against the center of a candle with painted numerals surrounding them for the face of the clock will help usher in the New Year and lend a cheerful glow to your party table.

An attractive bridge-luncheon centerpiece is made by cutting diamonds, hearts, spades and clubs from sheets of red and black beeswax and affixing them to the sides of a square white candle molded in a half-gallon milk carton. Small cookie cutters can be used to cut the shapes rapidly and evenly.

A wide variety of plastic molds are available for making poured wax appliqués to use in decorating candles. Some are large enough to cover the entire side of a candle (see Plate II); others are small and you may want to use several to decorate the candle (see Plate X), but be sure you measure the size of your candle and the size of the appliqué you choose to be sure it will fit. You can support these molds on several glasses or float them in water. Be sure they are level before filling. Oil the molds lightly and fill carefully and slowly, either with an eye dropper or from a tea kettle or coffee pot to avoid air bubbles. Refill as needed to make a flat back on your appliqué but do not permit the wax to build up into a hump. When the wax is solid gently flex the mold to remove the appliqué. If the appliqué is large it is easier and safer to turn it out onto a table and gently pull the mold up and away. Attach the appliqué to the candle by brushing a light coat of wax, melted to 230 degrees, on both the candle surface and the back of the appliqué. Work quickly and press the appliqué in place and hold it firmly until the wax has

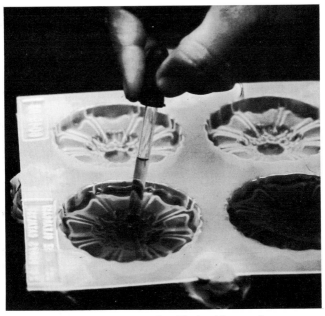

Small appliqué molds may be filled with eye dropper.

solidified. A wood-burning tool is helpful in filling and smoothing the seam between the appliqué and candle. There is no limit to the attractive and unusual candle designs that you can create by using the appliqué technique.

Beads, lace trims, sequins, jewels, artificial flowers, fruits and decals all find their place in candle decorating. The only rule when decorating with these is to keep inflammable materials well down on the candle so they do not interfere with burning, or plan to remove the decorations as the candle burns down to them. These decorations may be attached to the candle with glue, drops of melted wax or a supply of tiny straight pins available in hobby and craft shops. Regular-sized straight pins are too long and often crack off bits of the candle before they are completely inserted. Too many pins in a small area will also crack away part of the candle so they must be used judiciously. A thimble on the end of your thumb is helpful for pushing pins into the hard wax.

A most attractive candle is created by taking a plain, dark blue candle and trimming it with various-sized silver star sequins attached with tiny pins. Set the candle on a base of pale blue whipped wax and sprinkle with silver glitter.

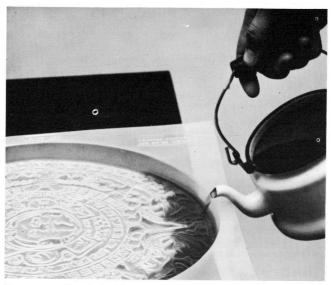

Larger appliqué molds may be filled with spout container.

Flex mold to remove wax shape.

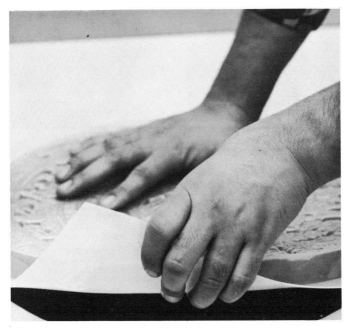

Turn larger molds out on table top.

Attach appliqué with melted wax.

Use a wood-burning tool to smooth seams.

A silver or gold numeral decal on the center of a tall, white milk-carton candle with a border of white whipped wax sprinkled with silver or gold glitter makes a lovely anniversary remembrance.

Decals or pictures cut from greeting cards or wrapping paper can be attached to the sides of a candle with wax melted to 230 degrees and brushed on. When the decal is in place dip the entire candle in a hot wax bath to give it an overall smooth finish, and an unusual and lovely candle will result.

Decals or pictures cut from greeting cards can be used for decoration.

Attach picture to candle with melted wax.

Give candle a hot wax bath to make a smooth finish.

A finished picture-decorated candle.

The combinations and designs are endless. Whatever the occasion, whatever the gift, you can make a candle uniquely beautiful and original. But suppose you want to expand your hobby into a profitable business venture, how do you get started? Read on.

9
Making Candlemaking Profitable

Many people who begin candlecrafting merely as a hobby soon find themselves, by accident or by intention, in the business of making candles for sale. This may happen simply because people who see your original designs are eager to have similar creations for their own enjoyment and quite naturally wish to reimburse you for materials and time. Or it may happen because you discover that in the joy of creating you end up with an oversupply and must find an outlet for your work if you are not to be inundated with candles.

The major problem in selling any handcrafted item is in establishing a fair price and yet one that will not put the product beyond the reach of prospective customers. Probably the easiest way to set prices is to visit the candle departments of several specialty and department stores in your area. Inspect the candles they have for sale, take notes on size, details and price and charge accordingly for your candles. In many cases you will find that you can command a higher price because handcrafted items always bring a better price than mass-produced products and your candles can be original, one-of-a-kind, often custom-created and decorated to a customer's specific order.

If there is no candle display available for comparison you should add up the cost of your materials, figure a sum for overhead (including electricity, cost of heating wax, water, work space), figure your time ($5 an hour is not excessive for the work of a skilled craftsman) and allow for a reasonable profit. Many retail stores figure a 100% markup on items they sell; this would mean you add all the above costs and then double that figure to come up with a fair selling price. On special and very unique candles you can often figure a much higher markup, as with the variegated spiral taper beeswax candle, which easily commands four to five times its cost.

Do not make the mistake of simply figuring in your $5 an hour and considering that sufficient profit. Remember that if your business expands to the point where you must hire additional help you will need to pay wages and yet as owner and operator of the business you are still entitled to some profit. There is also the time spent in business-connected activities such as telephoning, bookkeeping and ordering of supplies, which you do not figure into the cost of the individual candle but is covered by your overall markup figure.

But suppose you have not reached the point where word of mouth advertising and demand keeps you as busy as you would like to be. How can you obtain more orders to increase your business and profits?

One way is to approach small businesses in your area with samples. A few months before Christmas is an excellent time to approach the buyer in department stores and specialty shops, as candles are one of their biggest sellers for this holiday. Your local pharmacy may be willing to place a display for you. Florists are another good prospect. The proprietor may only be willing to give you space for a display with your phone number for customers to call and order direct from you. Or he may wish to place an order for a specific number of candles to be sold by him "on consignment." This means he puts the candles on display and pays you for them only after they are sold. This is a bit risky as candles can be damaged and you often bear the loss. But if it is the only way to gain advertising it is better than none.

The best way is to obtain a definite order for candles to be purchased outright by the store (at a price less than what you would get from the customer direct of course) and sold by the store at a profit. Many candlecrafters have established a most profitable business this way with the better department stores.

An excellent way to obtain publicity that will only cost you a few pennies is to donate a large special candle to a local church or organizational bazaar. When you make arrangements for your donation specify that the candle is to be displayed in a prominent place along with your name, address and telephone number. Many of these organizations take bids, sell raffle tickets or use such a candle as a door prize and therefore it need not be taken off display until the end of the affair and provides excellent publicity for you.

You can hold a candle display "open house" in your own home. Advertise in the newspaper and by word of mouth. Posters about town are another way of getting the word out. Arrange all your candles attractively in whatever areas you decide to use. A living and dining room with table tops, extra card-tables and all available surfaces covered with a variety of candles, many of them lit, makes a most intriguing display. Supply coffee and tea and tiny cookies for refreshments in one corner. Take orders early in your display. Near the end you may want to sell the candles as people ask for them. Such an open house is especially good if held six to eight weeks before Christmas.

Donating small and simply decorated candles to a local hospital or convalescent home or to your church shut-ins at Christmas time often pays handsome dividends in inner satisfaction as well as future orders for special candles. Attach a small label with your name and phone number on the bottom of each candle.

When turning a hobby to profit one often overlooked source of income is in demonstrations. Club and social groups are always looking for something different for entertainment and women's groups especially welcome a demonstration of candlemaking.

Arranging such a demonstration requires some advance planning. As time is usually limited to an hour or so for the total demonstration you will need to prepare beforehand a candle that is cured and ready to be removed from its mold. Another candle poured just an hour or so before the demonstration so it is solidified enough to demonstrate refilling should also be ready.

You might begin your demonstration by setting up your equipment—a hot plate will do for a heat source—showing safety precautions and starting your wax to melt. Next demonstrate how a milk carton is prepared for use as a candle mold. Include information on proper waxes, wicks, temperatures, colors and scents.

Demonstrate the pouring of the mold. Then show the previously poured candle with its indentation ready for refilling. Demonstrate the refilling process, explaining the importance of this step to the proper burning of the candle. Set this mold aside and show the completely cured candle and demonstrate its removal from the mold. It might be wise to have this candle chilled so you encounter no difficulty in removing it from the mold.

At this point it is fun to demonstrate the whipped wax technique. Usually the wax you have melted first will be about the right temperature for whipping. Using the whipped wax make a base, decorate the candle you have removed from the mold, add a few decorations and glitter you have brought along for this purpose and present the finished creation to what will probably be an entranced audience.

If time permits you may go on to demonstrate the easily made beeswax taper. Many demonstrators find that their audience likes to join with them in making this simple candle.

It is best to inquire of the program chairman at the time you contract for the demonstration as to whether the group would like to participate in this activity. If so, you could make up small packets in advance containing a triangular piece of beeswax, a length of wick, and a bit of glitter, all neatly packaged in a plastic bag. It is best to use small triangles of beeswax for this project as they are more easily managed by beginners and it may not be possible for everyone to have a table surface on which to work. The tiny two-inch Christmas trees are an excellent project and can even be rolled quite adequately using a firm magazine on one's lap for a table surface. Using half-sheets of beeswax cut into triangles to make eight-inch tapers also works well. Make a charge for your packets including a small profit of ten cents or so to cover the time you spent preparing them and pass them out to those who wish to participate. A Christmas tree packet could probably be handled for fifteen to twenty-five cents and the larger taper packets for twenty-five to thirty-five cents each.

You would of course receive a fee for your time, usually about ten to fifteen dollars. Not only are you paid for your time but you are gaining valuable publicity for your own creations, and arranging a display of your specialties for the members to look at before and after the demonstration and offering them for sale or taking orders pays off handsomely.

These demonstrations often lead to requests for classes in candlemaking, and establishing classes is no more difficult than preparing for a demonstration. You will need to decide how many classes you wish to offer in your series and which candles and techniques you want to teach to your students. The material in this book should make an excellent guide.

If you have space to allow it, arranging for each student to make the candle during class time is an excellent method. You are right on hand to offer advice and correct errors. But most of the time you will probably find a lecture-demonstration type of lesson works better. In this the students take notes and then try the techniques at home before the next lesson, bringing in their questions and problems the next time for your help.

The exceptions of course are the beeswax candles, which are so easily made as a group project. Here again, making yourself available to school, church, scout and civic organizations to lead an afternoon or evening project in making beeswax candles is an excellent way to publicize your products and also bring in added income. You may charge for your services or, as is more common in this type of program, you may supply the materials for the project, allowing yourself a small profit on each item.

As you instruct more people in candlemaking you will find more coming to you for materials. Many candlecrafters have established a successful sideline business in selling candlemaking materials along with their finished products.

To do this you would find it most profitable to make arrangements with a nearby supplier so you purchase from him in quantity at discount and then resell the items at a profit.

In all these business plans you must remember your responsibility to federal and state governments. It is necessary that you keep careful records of expenses and income. You are allowed tax deductions for legitimate business expenses such as equipment, use of space and utilities in your home and transportation. Some locations require you to have a license to resell supplies of any sort or to sell the products you create. Information about such regulations is usually available at your city hall or your state capitol. The public library offers a number of books and pamphlets on running a small business and you may find it wise to consult an accountant for the best system of bookkeeping for your enterprise.

Whether you are candlemaking for fun or for profit you will need a source of supply. Often local hobby shops carry supplies but stocks are frequently low except before Christmas and most candlecrafters find they must have a larger variety and more constant source of supply. The major petroleum companies manufacture candle wax as a by-product of the petroleum industry and you can telephone or write their headquarters for information about their product and local availability. The Standard Oil Company offers candle wax formulated in four melting points, and delivery to your home or a service station nearby can sometimes be arranged. Prices are most reasonable. Obtain the address of the distribution center nearest you from your service station if none is listed in your telephone directory and write for information.

Remember that postage will increase your expenses so try to locate a source of supply as nearby as possible. The following list includes supply houses in all parts of the country and there are undoubtedly many more.

Mail-order Candle Supply Houses

Pourette Manufacturing Co.
8818 Roosevelt Way. N.E.
Seattle, Wash. 98115

Triarce Arts & Crafts
Dept. M-8 P.O. Box 106
Northfield, Ill. 60093

The Glow Candle Co.
17 West 39th St.
P.O. Box 5817
Kansas City, Mo.

American Handicrafts Co.
18-20 W. 14th St.
New York, N.Y.
(Branches in most major cities)

Kit Kraft
12109 Ventura Pl.
Studio City, Calif. 91604

Premier Manf. Co.
P.O. Box 26126
Denver, Colorado 80226

Lee Wards
840 North State St. (Rt. 31)
Elgin, Illinois 60121

General Supplies Co.
P.O. Box 338
Fallbrook, Calif. 92028

Candlelite House
4228 E. Easter Place
Littleton, Colorado 80120

Wicks & Wax Candle Shop
350 N. Atlantic Avenue
Cocoa Beach, Florida 32931

Cake Decorators & Crafts
Supplies
Blacklick, Ohio 43004

Maid of Scandinavia Co.
3245 Raleigh Ave.
Minneapolis, Minn. 55416

Frank B. Ross Co. Inc.
6 Ash Street
Jersey City, New Jersey

Lumi-Craft (Canada) Ltd.
P.O. Box 666
Kingston, Ontario, Canada

Myart Co. Pty. Ltd.
Box 3966 G.P.O.
Sydney, New South Wales
Australia

Camp-O-Matic Ltd.
P.O. Box 21
Lansdowne
Capetown, South Africa

10
Questions and Answers

CAN STORE-BOUGHT CANDLES BE MELTED DOWN?
Yes. Scrape away any particles of dirt or charred wick. When the wax is melted you may need to strain it through a filter such as is described for making the memento candle in Chapter 7.

CAN REMNANTS OF OLD CANDLES BE MELTED DOWN AND REUSED? Yes, but it is best to melt colors separately or you will most likely end up with an unattractive dirty-brown color. These are also good for breaking up and using in marbleized candles.

CAN BENT TAPERS BE STRAIGHTENED? Yes. Place them in a container of warm (not hot) water for about five to ten minutes until they become pliable. Remove from the water and quickly roll them on a cold, hard surface such as a piece of glass or a formica counter top.

IS IT POSSIBLE TO REUNITE BROKEN TAPERS? Sometimes. You might try brushing the broken ends with hot (230 degrees) melted wax and pressing them together. Covering them with whipped wax, bands of gold foil or strips of wax will provide extra stability. Larger-diameter candles are more readily reunited than slender tapers because of the larger area that can be waxed and joined.

HOW SHOULD WAX BE CLEANED FROM UTENSILS? While the utensil is still hot pour the wax out and wipe quickly with a paper towel, then wash in hot, soapy water. Small utensils can be boiled in a pan of water. The wax will melt and float to the top; when the water cools, the wax will solidify on top and can be picked off the surface, and the utensils lifted out.

HOW CAN MOLDS BE CLEANED WHEN BITS OF WAX REMAIN? Metal molds can be placed on a piece of paper toweling in an oven no warmer than 175 degrees. Tilt the bottom up slightly for drainage and leave in the oven for about 15 minutes. Chemical cleaners are available at candle supply shops. You can also pour the next candle with wax at about 230 degrees and the bits of wax will be melted off and absorbed. For plastic molds, place in quite warm water, allow wax to soften then wipe out the mold.

CAN WAX BE REMOVED FROM FABRICS? Sometimes. Scrape as much of the wax off the fabric as possible. If the fabric is washable, place paper toweling over the wax spot and press with a warm iron until no more wax melts out of the material. Hold the material under hot running water to remove any remaining wax and launder as usual. Sometimes several treatments will be needed. For nonwashable fabrics, after scraping wax off, take the garment to your dry cleaner and be sure to tell him what has made the spot. Wax on carpets or furniture can usually be removed by the paper towel and iron method.

HOW SHOULD OLD WAX BE DISPOSED OF? It is rare that you will have wax to throw away because most can be melted down, filtered and reused. But should you accidentally scorch the wax, making it unfit for use, pour it into an empty tin can or milk carton, allow it to harden and dispose of it in the garbage or incinerator. *Never* pour wax down the drain; a costly plumbing bill will be your reward.

CAN BEESWAX BE MIXED WITH OTHER WAXES?
Yes. It greatly improves the burning qualities of paraffin. See
Chapter 2 for formulas.

CAN WICKS FROM OTHER CANDLES BE REUSED?
I assume you mean unburned candles, as wicks are consumed
in the burning process. Yes. Melt the candle down, fish the
wick out of the liquid wax and lay it straight out on a
piece of waxed paper to dry. Use as you would any other
wick.

WHAT IS THE BEST WAY TO STORE CANDLES?
Candles must be stored in a cool, dust-free location; most
kitchen cupboards are taboo. Wrapping each candle in plastic
wrap and cushioning well with crumpled tissue or newspaper
should keep them free from dust and prevent marks on the
surface. Be sure the area is away from radiators, heating or
hot-water pipes and heat of the summer sun.

WHAT IS THE BEST WAY TO SHIP CANDLES? Again,
wrap well with plastic wrap, cushion with tissue, newspaper
or excelsior and wrap securely. Bulky candles usually travel
well. Delicate ones should be sent "special handling." And a
label warning "Keep Away From Heat—Handle With Care"
should be attached, though it does not always insure safe
arrival.

WHAT ARE THE MOST USED SCENTS FOR CAN-
DLES? Rose, pine, gardenia, lilac and bayberry, in my own
experience.

HOW MUCH SCENT IS NEEDED FOR HOW MUCH
WAX? This depends on individual preference of course, but
in general one-quarter- to one-half-teaspoonful per pound
of wax should be sufficient.

CAN CONTAINER-TYPE CANDLES BE REFILLED?
Certainly. The big difficulty lies in removing any remaining
old wax and the old wick holder. Pouring hot water into the
container or submerging the container in hot water often
loosens the wax so it can be lifted out. A piece of wire
coathanger with a little hook made at one end may help you
reach into the tall, thin glass containers to pull the wax out.

Remove the little metal wick tab that is usually used in these, clean the wax off of it and reuse it to hold your wick. You will want to use a wire wick and a low-melting-point wax for refilling.

I REFILLED A CONTAINER CANDLE FOR A FRIEND AND NOW UNMELTED WAX STICKS TO THE INSIDE OF THE CONTAINER. WHY? You may have used too high a melting-point wax; the flame does not provide enough heat to the outer edges of the wax and they do not have an opportunity to melt away. Try burning the candle for a longer period of time. This may increase the temperature inside the container and melt away a larger area of wax.

WHAT DOES *SPLAY* MEAN WHEN REFERRING TO A CANDLE? This refers to the action of some waxes when the candle is burning. Instead of melting and being consumed, or running down the side of the candle, the wax softens and bends away from the candle in large foliating sheets. This is often considered desirable, and chemicals to make this happen are available from candle supply houses.

WHAT MAKES MY CANDLES SPIT WAX WHILE BURNING? This is usually a result of air pockets formed around the wick when the candle was curing which were not punctured and filled. Air trapped in these pockets expands when heated by the candle flame, then bursts through the thin wax film of the pocket and splatters the melted wax puddled around the wick.

I HAVE TROUBLE GETTING MY CANDLES OUT OF THE METAL MOLDS. WHAT CAN I DO TO CORRECT THIS? Be sure you allow the candles to cure for a least eight hours; as wax cools it contracts and pulls away from the sides. You might try refrigerating for half an hour, but do not leave the mold in the refrigerator too long or the candle may crack. Be careful not to let wax run down between the hardening candle and the side of the mold when you are refilling. You might also try cleaning the molds and using a silicone spray. Sometimes simply changing to a higher-melting-point or a different supply of wax helps.

MY CANDLES OFTEN HAVE CHALKY MARKS THAT
LOOK LIKE FROST ON THE SURFACE. WHAT
CAUSES THIS? The wax may have been at too low a temperature when it was poured. Try pouring with wax at least
180 degrees. Warming the mold before pouring and using
a water bath may also help eliminate this.

MY CANDLES HAVE TINY PITS ON THE SURFACE.
WHY? You may have poured with the wax too hot. Never
pour wax over 210 degrees unless you must do so for some
special reason. Too-slow cooling in hot weather may also
be to blame. Try using a water bath. Pouring wax into the
mold too fast will also cause this by creating small air bubbles
on the surface.

THE SIDES OF MY HURRICANE CANDLE SAGGED
AFTER BURNING. WHY? You may have used too low a
melting-point wax for the shell. Be sure the wax for a
hurricane shell is 140 to 150 degrees melting point. The
votive light inside should be in a glass container, and low-
melting-point (125-degree) wax should be used for this. A
hurricane candle shell should be at least four inches across
so that the votive light is not too close to the sides. Be sure
it is centered in the candle and do not burn hurricane candles
in a draft which may throw too much heat to one side. Do
not burn for too long a time. Check the sides occasionally;
if they are getting soft put out the flame until the shell
hardens again. Do not let the votive light burn all the way to
the bottom of the glass or it may melt through the bottom of
the hurricane shell.

IS THERE A MEANING ASSOCIATED WITH DIF-
FERENT CANDLE COLORS? Symbolic meanings have
long been given to colors but there is wide variation in these
meanings. Different cultures and religions attribute different
meanings to colors. In Chinese art, colors have symbolic
meaning only when combined with one another; for example:

Black on red: happiness   Red on green: happiness
Gold on red: special happiness   Red on yellow: loyalty
Black on yellow: religiousness   White on red: good luck
Gold on white: aristocracy   Yellow on white: holiness

In the Christian religion the Trinity is represented as blue for God, red for the Holy Ghost and yellow for Jesus the Son. The same three colors are also used to represent heaven, hell and earth, or the spirit of man, the body of man, the mind of man. Freemasonry uses blue, purple, red and white as their colors, and the same colors were used by the Hebrews to represent Jehovah.

Red has been said to have magical powers to ward off sickness and evil while others claim it has the power to bring love. Black is the color of revenge while white represents purity, peace, prayer. Blue stands for loyalty and friendship and green is often used to represent immortality and prosperity.

Marie Laveau, a famed Voodoo queen of the mid-1800s, used the following zodiacal colors in practicing her art.

Aries:	pink and orange	Libra:	pink and old gold
Taurus:	blue and old gold	Scorpio:	yellow and blue
Gemini:	red and blue	Sagittarius:	red and orange
Cancer:	red and green	Capricorn:	red and old gold
Leo:	pink and orange	Aquarius:	yellow and blue
Virgo:	pink and old gold	Pisces:	blue and green

WHEN CUSTOMERS ORDER DUPLICATE CANDLES I HAVE GREAT DIFFICULTY DUPLICATING THE EXACT COLOR. SOME CUSTOMERS HAVE BEEN DISAPPOINTED WHEN THE COLOR THEY RECEIVED WAS DIFFERENT· FROM WHAT THEY HAD EXPECTED. IS THERE ANYTHING I CAN DO TO MAKE MY COLORS MORE CONSTANT? It is very difficult to duplicate a candle color exactly. Wax colors are rather like dye lots in yarn and material and vary from lot to lot. But you can come reasonably close if you are willing to take the trouble to measure carefully and keep accurate records. First, make a mark on your melting pot to indicate the level of melted wax you will use. Always have your wax full to this line and at the same temperature when adding color. For more accurate measuring, the liquid candle dyes are easiest to use. Use a medicine dropper (a child's vitamin dropper with marks on the side is great) and carefully write down the amount of each color dye used. Also keep track of the type of wax used, any additions of stearic acid, luster crystals, etc., as these also affect the finished color. You will then be able to approximate the color more easily.

Your customers will find a color wheel helpful in choosing colors. A white paper plate with a plastic finish is good. It can be hung up with a string through a hole in the edge, or a tack through the center will permit it to turn. Use two of them, and as you formulate each of your colors drop a blob of the colored wax on each plate. Carefully note the amounts of wax and dye, and on one of the color wheels carefully note this information beside each color sample. On the other wheel, the one your customers will use to select colors, use a number or special name for each color. Then when Mrs. Nelson calls back to order another set of those "lovely sunset-pink pillars" you will be able to duplicate the color just as nearly as is possible.

HINT: Candles burning in a room will help eliminate cigarette odors and smoke.

CAN PLASTIC-FOAM CUPS BE USED AS MOLDS? Yes, I have used them successfully. Some plastic-foam cups may not be satisfactory, but the ones designed for use with hot beverages work well for me. You can pour the wax at temperatures from 165 to 190 degrees, and the candles release easily even when the cup has not been oiled. The surface of the candle is covered with a fine, lacelike, webbed design which adds interest rather than being objectionable.

IS THERE AN ORGANIZATION OF ANY SORT WHERE CANDLE HOBBYISTS CAN GET TOGETHER AND SHARE IDEAS? Yes. The International Guild of Candle Artisans was formed in 1965. Two years ago there were 125 members, today they have some 700 members in 49 states, Bermuda, Canada, New Zealand and Greece. They hold a convention each summer, have regional workshops and publish a monthly newsletter, *The Candlelighter*, filled with hints and ideas. Small groups exchange round-robin letters with ideas, problems and solutions. If you are interested in joining or would like more information write to the president, Mrs. Dorothy Anglin, 16 Morningside, S.E., Grand Rapids, Michigan 49506.

Index

Joan Ann Unger

In the early 1960s, living too far from a hospital to practice nursing, Joan Ann Unger took a candlemaking course. This quickly led to demonstrations in the craft and finally to teaching classes. *Creative Candlecraft* grew out of her own enjoyment and experience with the hobby, the notes she had evolved for her classes and her newfound joy of writing for publication.

Married twenty years, Michigan-born Indiana-raised Joan Ann Unger enjoys a variety of handicrafts, from ceramics to knitting, and cans and freezes produce from the family's own half-acre garden (bounded by almost 4000 serene acres of state recreational land which is, as she says, "delightful for writing!"). A travel and camping buff, she enthusiastically shares her sportsman husband's current dream of a camping trip to Alaska, and proudly numbers, among the rest of her family, a daughter, a son, two Golden Retrievers and a Yorkshire Terrier.